Noah Down the Stairs

Lyrics by
Tony Kushner

Music by
Jeanine Tesori

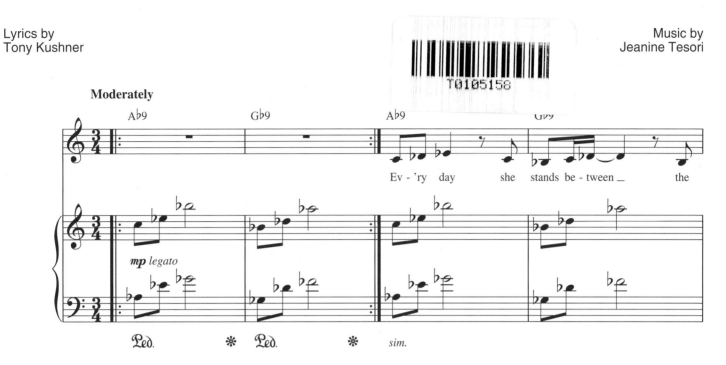

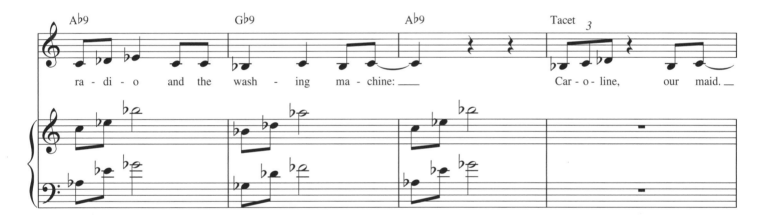

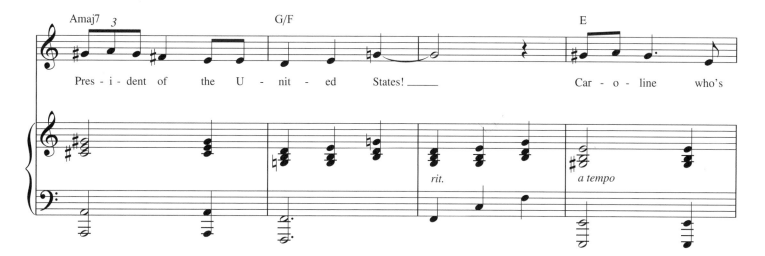

Pres - i - dent of the U - nit - ed States! _____ Car - o - line who's

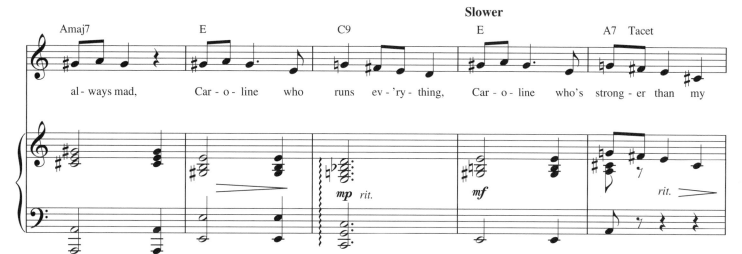

Slower

al - ways mad, Car - o - line who runs ev - 'ry - thing, Car - o - line who's strong - er than my

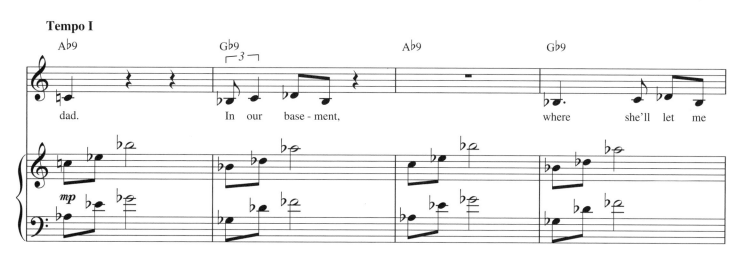

Tempo I

dad. In our base - ment, where she'll let me

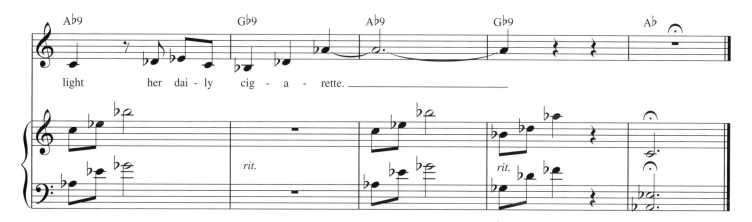

light her dai - ly cig - a - rette. _____

I Got Four Kids

Lyrics by
Tony Kushner

Music by
Jeanine Tesori

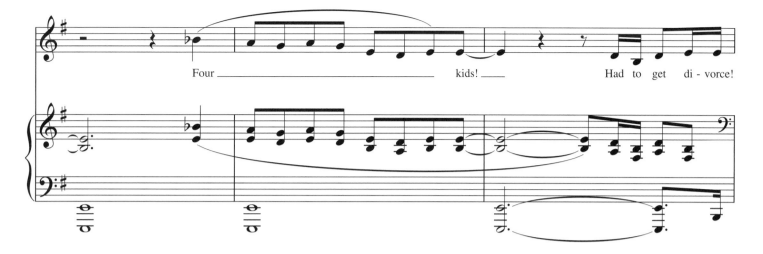

Four _____ kids! _____ Had to get di - vorce!

The Dryer:
Oh, _____ oh. _____

Ah. *Caroline:* Been twen - ty - two years of clean - ing. For all them

years I worked __ and prayed. _____ Ev - 'ry day ___ I do - in' laun -

nine - teen six - ty - three _ and I,   I wish ev - 'ry af - ter - noon _ I die: _

(Groan)   *(Cry)*

_____ Cook and clean _ and mind that boy, _ do - in' house-

Mm, _____ mm, _____

work, do - in' laun - dry six - teen feet be - low _

mm, _____ mm. Ah oo, _____ ah oo, _____ ah

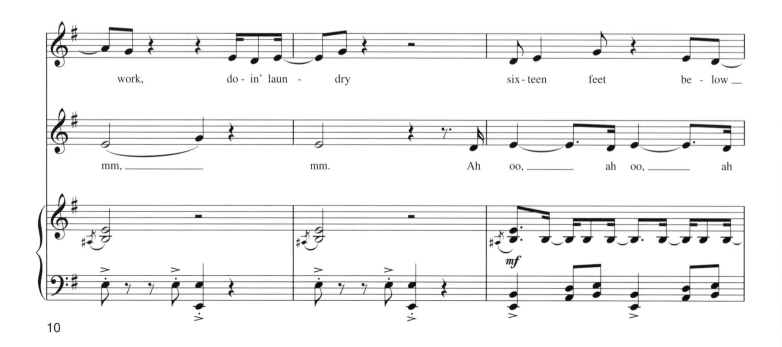

_the sea. ___ Thought for sure by now ___ I be ___

oo, _cha,_ ah oo. ___ Ah oo, _cha,_ ah oo, _cha,_ ah oo, _cha,_ ah oo. ___

Am7   G/B   C

some - place cool - er,   some - place high, ___   some - place where they's

sub. **mp** _colla voce_

Bm   Am7   G/B

some - thing dry ___   don't come from no 'lec - tric dry - er.

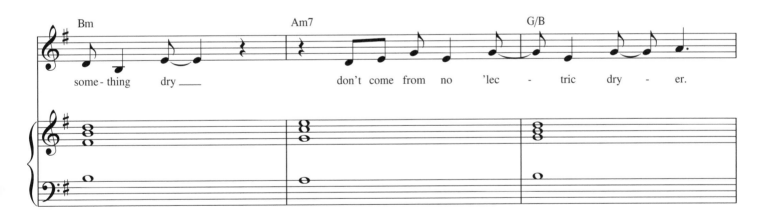

C7   Bm   C7

Do - in' some - thing fin - er,   some - thing not as

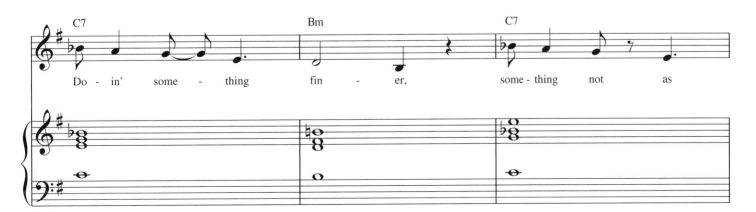

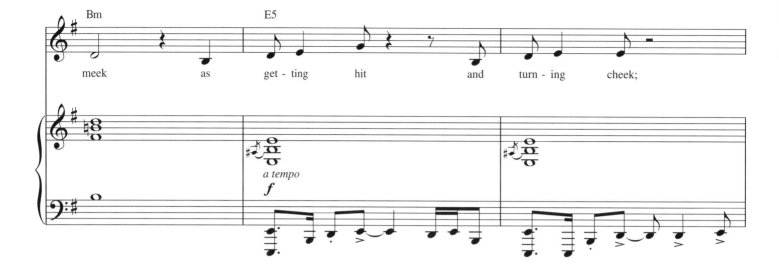

meek as get - ting hit and turn - ing cheek;

Caroline: hit! and turn the oth - er cheek. __ Hit! and turn the oth -

Dryer: Huh! *Huh!*

er cheek, __ do - in' laun - dry un - der - ground for

oo, *ch,* ah oo, *ch,* ah oo, *ch,* ah oo, *ch,* ah

The Dryer, The Washing Machine:

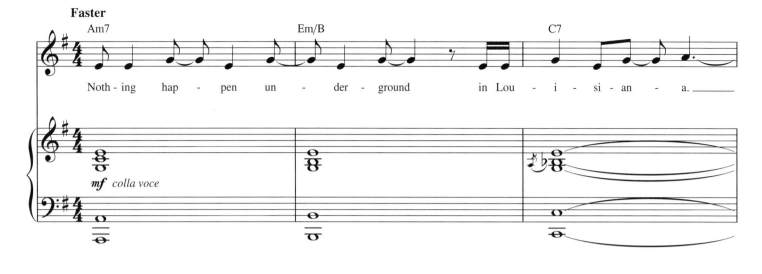

Noth - ing hap - pen un - der - ground in Lou - i - si - an - a.

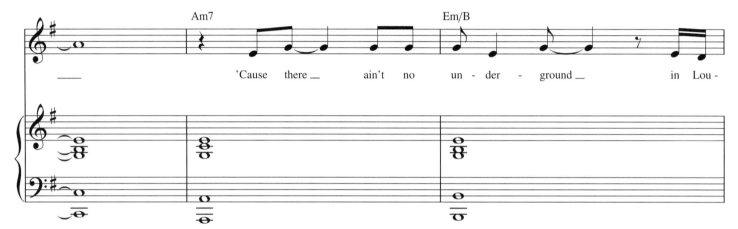

'Cause there ___ ain't no un - der - ground ___ in Lou -

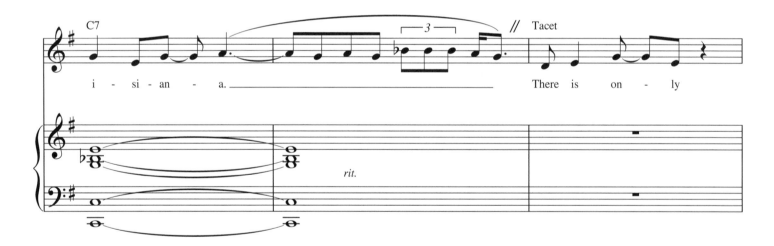

i - si - an - a. ___ There is on - ly

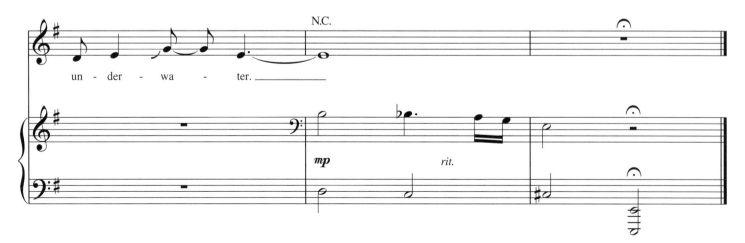

un - der - wa - ter. ___

Long Distance

Words by
Tony Kushner

Music by
Jeanine Tesori

15

I'm fine, just fine, I'm learn-ing the lin-go: Mag-

Slower

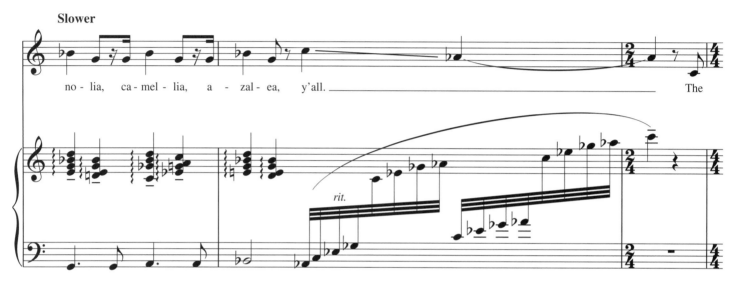

no - lia, ca - mel - lia, a - zal - ea, y'all. _____ The

tem - ple, *get this,* has Sun - day night bin - go just like the goy - im.

Faster   **A tempo**

Oy.   A long ___ dis - tance call! So much to tell. The

boy still hates me. *I really shouldn't be talking so loud.* He leaves mon - ey in his pock - ets, and

that real - ly grates me. I tell him and tell him it's not al - lowed, just

shuck - ing your laun - dry *—You hear that? "Shuck!" I'm a southerner already—* on - to the floor;

take the mon - ey out first, __ God knows we're not poor, but show re - spect for your fa - ther. He worked

Faster

spoiled _ and qui - et; sad, I guess. I'm on a di - et. I

bought a new dress. Stu's giv - ing les - sons, play - ing,

Freely

do - ing fine: the work is stead - y. He still miss - es Bet - ty. I don't mind. __

__ I miss her, too. She was my best friend. I miss the

cit - y. I miss the old crowd.

What? Because we haven't got—We can't give her a raise!
Pa! We aren't rich, we're just plain folk,
we've only got bupkes ourselves—we're broke!

Typical you obsess about the maid while your daughter's miserable.

No, not miserable, I never said—

Well, it's not what I meant.

I'm just not... Just not...

Slowly

a hun-dred per - cent. It's ver - y hot, and ver - y

damp, and out in the back-yard there's a lit-tle swamp.

Full of nois-y frogs. Last night I cried. I

miss you, Pa. I miss the Up-per West Side.

Moon Change

Words by
Tony Kushner

Music by
Jeanine Tesori

Moon Trio

Words by
Tony Kushner

Music by
Jeanine Tesori

The Moon: Moon change, moon change, glow-ing bright,

I'm wait-in' here in - stead. _____

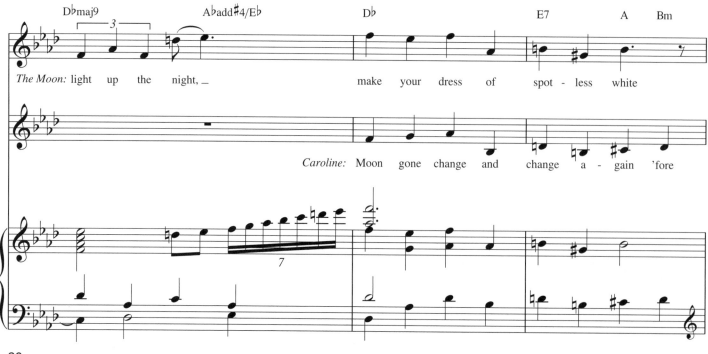

The Moon: light up the night, ___ make your dress of spot-less white

Caroline: Moon gone change and change a - gain 'fore

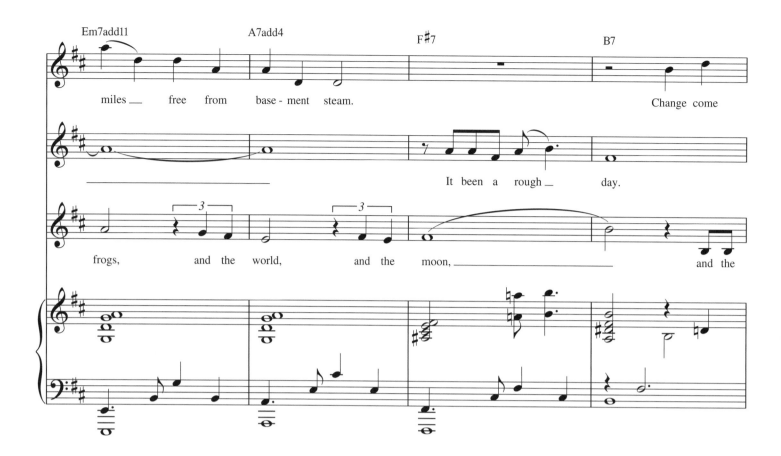

miles __ free from base - ment steam.

It been a rough __ day.

frogs, and the world, and the moon, __ and the

Change come

fast, __ change come slow, but change __

I put all that a - way. __

sky __ go from cloud - y to clear. __

Times

The Bus

Words by
Tony Kushner

Music by
Jeanine Tesori

*Crash against low black and white keys with right forearm.

32

No One Waitin'/'Night Mama

Words by
Tony Kushner

Music by
Jeanine Tesori

No One Waitin'
Slow and bluesy, in 4

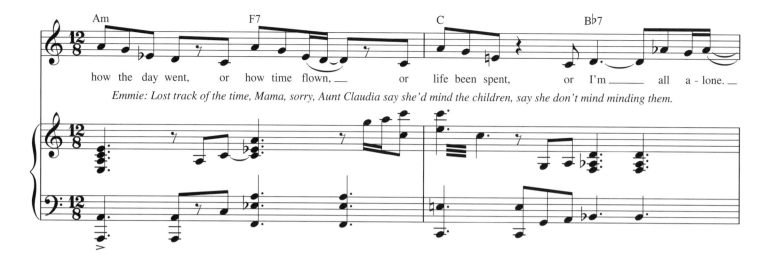

how the day went, or how time flown, ___ or life been spent, or I'm ___ all a - lone. ___

Emmie: Lost track of the time, Mama, sorry, Aunt Claudia say she'd mind the children, say she don't mind minding them.

___ Sorry, Mama, I was out, being shiftless, having fun. *Caroline: What kind of fun?*

Fast

Emmie: You re - mem - ber fun, Ma - ma,

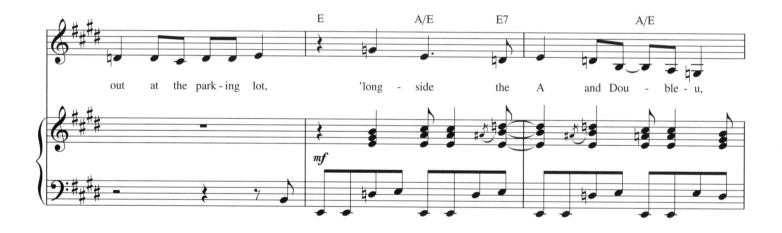

out at the park - ing lot, 'long - side the A and Dou - ble - u,

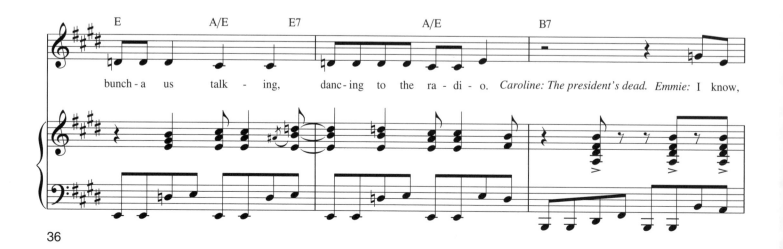

bunch - a us talk - ing, danc - ing to the ra - di - o. *Caroline: The president's dead. Emmie: I know,*

man...   *Caroline: Emmie Thibodeaux! Since when you say black man? Say colored or Negro, like you was raised up to.*

Ah -

Emmie: Say he do _____ stuff for _____ us,   get our vote,

ooh.   Ah - ooh.

he just ig - nore   us,   same old sto - ry, Ma - ma,

Same old sto - ry, Ma - ma,

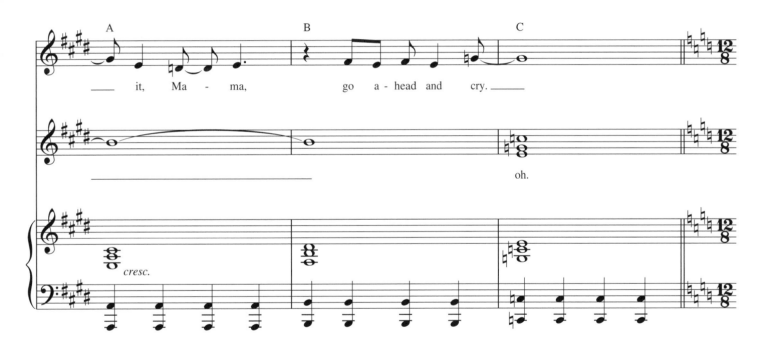

Tempo I

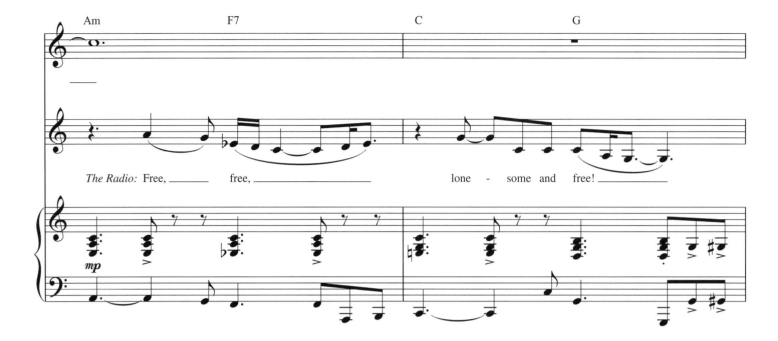

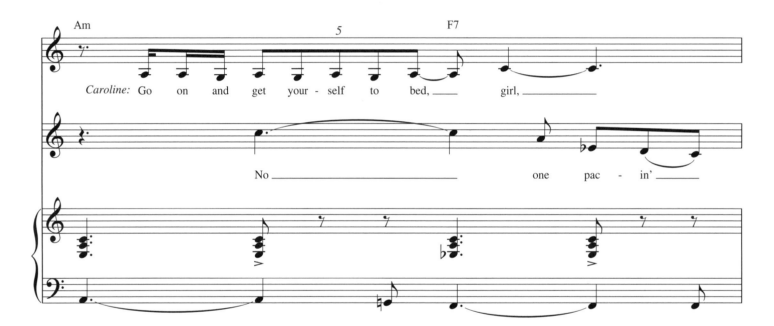

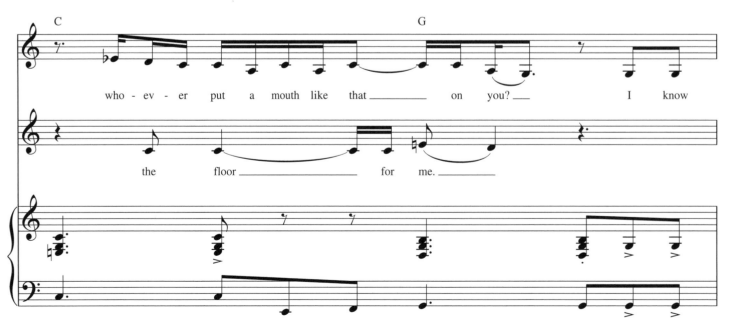

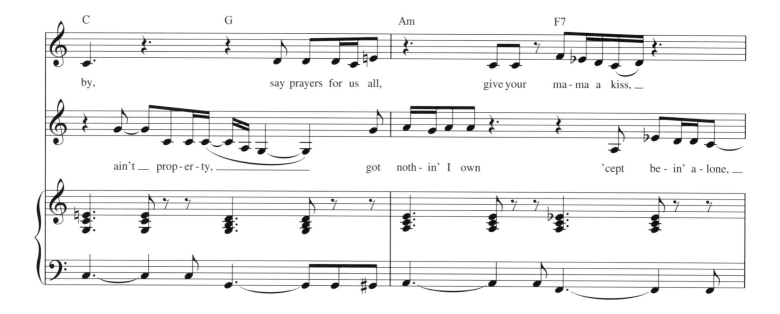

by, say prayers for us all, give your ma-ma a kiss, __

ain't __ prop-er-ty, _____ got noth-in' I own 'cept be-in' a-lone, __

'pol-o-gize to God for be-ing such a un-ho-ly priss, and a cau-tion, and a sass,

free and lone - ly... _____

'Night Mama

Moderately, in 2

Emmie:

'fore your ma-ma whups your... 'Night, Ma-ma! 'Night, God! _ 'Night, ra-di-o!

mp legato

42

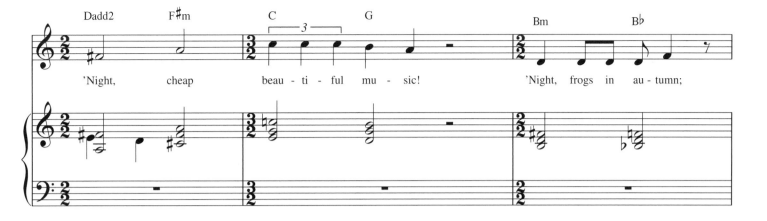

'Night, cheap beau-ti-ful mu-sic! 'Night, frogs in au-tumn;

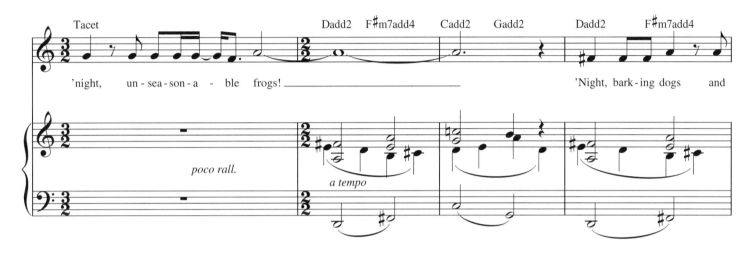

'night, un-sea-son-a-ble frogs! _____ 'Night, bark-ing dogs and

poco rall.   *a tempo*

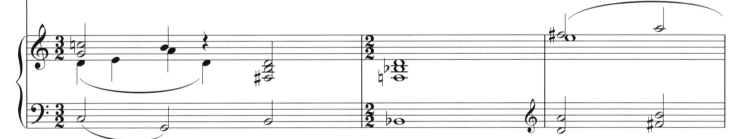

mice-hunt-ing cats and ci-ca-das in the pe-can trees, and ev-'ry-thing that dies when

win-ter comes! 'Night, light-ning bugs! Good night! _____

poco rall.   *a tempo*

Gonna Pass Me a Law/Noah, Go to Sleep

Words by
Tony Kushner

Music by
Jeanine Tesori

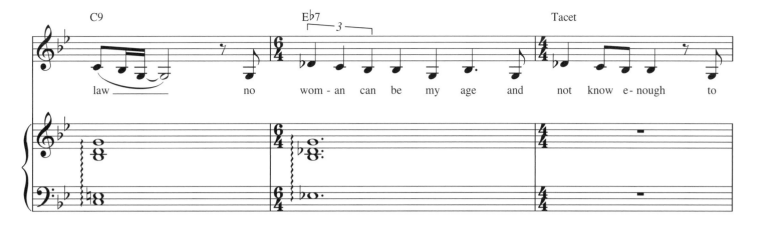

law _____ no wom-an can be my age and not know e-nough to

Moderately, with a Latin feel

read a _____ map. Gon-na pass me a law _____ that my

heath-en _____ daugh-ter don't nev-er get hurt nor learn how to mind _____ me, nor

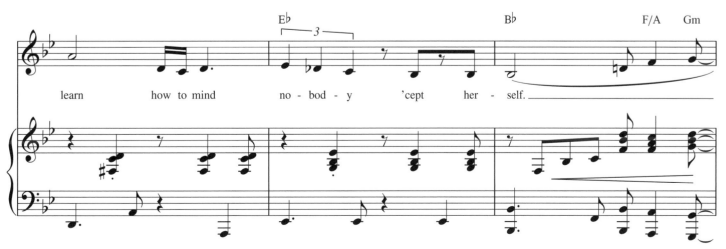

learn how to mind no-bod-y 'cept her-self. _____

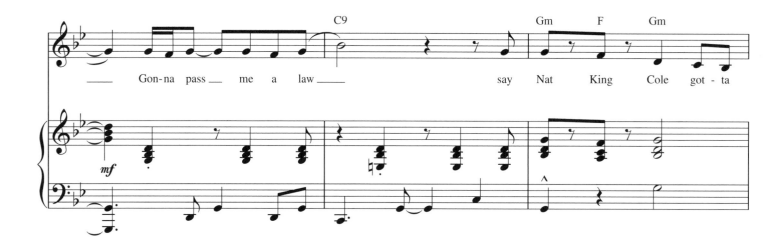

Gon-na pass ___ me a law ___ say Nat King Cole got-ta

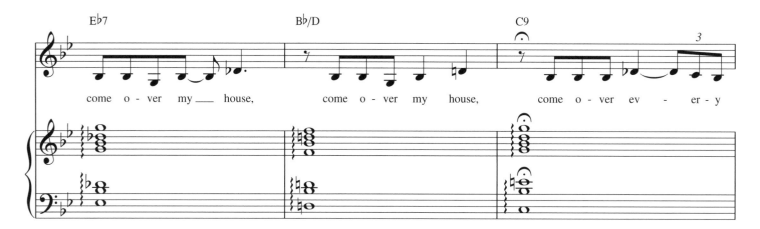

come o - ver my ___ house, come o - ver my house, come o - ver ev - er - y

Noah, Go to Sleep
Freely

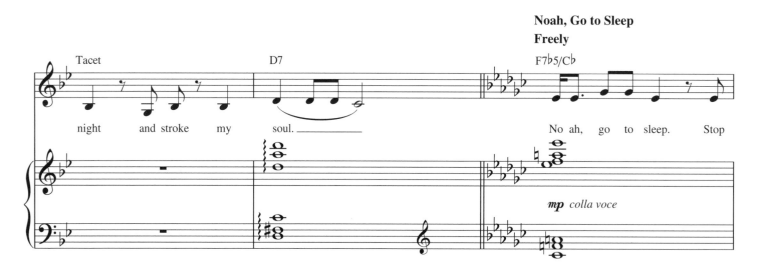

night and stroke my soul. ___ No ah, go to sleep. Stop

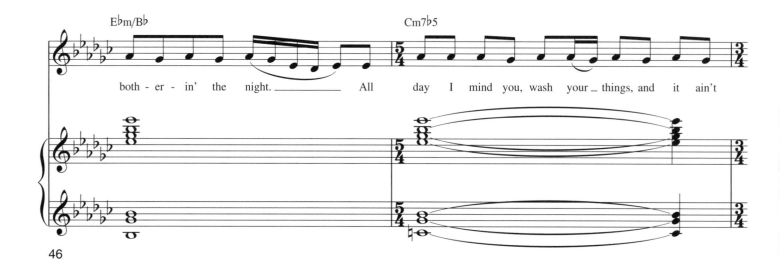

both - er - in' the night. ___ All day I mind you, wash your ___ things, and it ain't

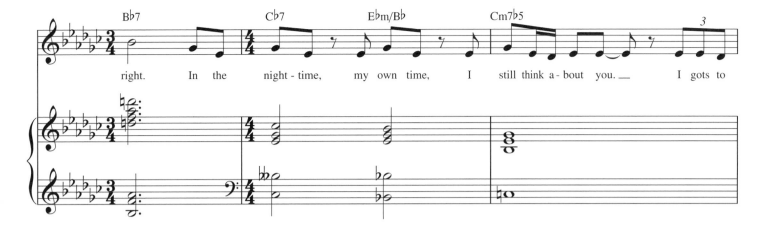

right. In the night-time, my own time, I still think a-bout you. __ I gots to

Moderately, in 2

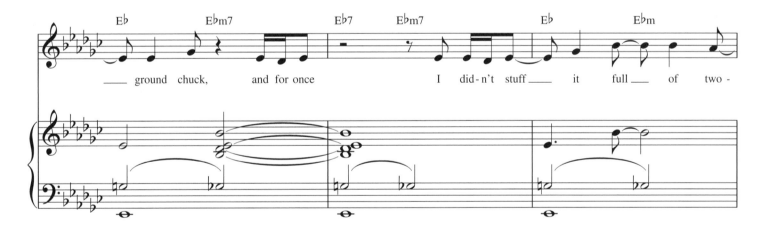

think a-bout rent o-ver-due, _____ 'cause last week twice I bought __

rall. *mp a tempo*

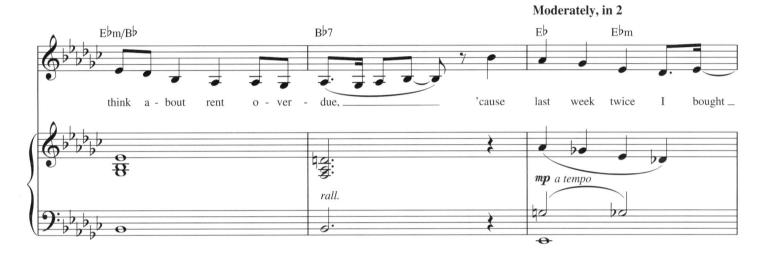

__ ground chuck, and for once I did-n't stuff __ it full __ of two-

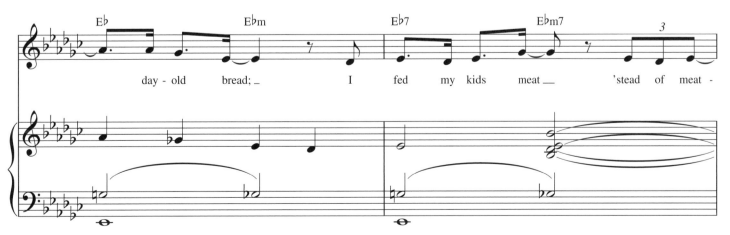

day-old bread; __ I fed my kids meat __ 'stead of meat-

Slower

Roosevelt Petrucius Coleslaw

Words by
Tony Kushner

Music by
Jeanine Tesori

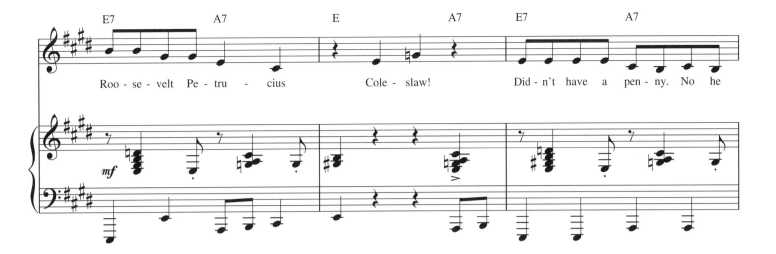

Roo - se - velt Pe - tru - cius Cole - slaw! Did - n't have a pen - ny. No he

did - n't have an - y. So he ask his ma, __ Old La - dy Cole - slaw!

"Ma, I'm broke __ and Ma, I'm glum!" __ And Glo - ry Hal - le - lu - jah to King -

dom Come! __ Ma reach in her pock - ets and she give him some!

+ Joe, Jackie:

Emmie: "Look here, Roo-se-velt, see here, Ro! __ I got a pen-ny!"

Joe, Jackie: "No, Ma-ma, no!" Emmie: "I gots a nick-el." Joe, Jackie: "Won't buy a pick-le!

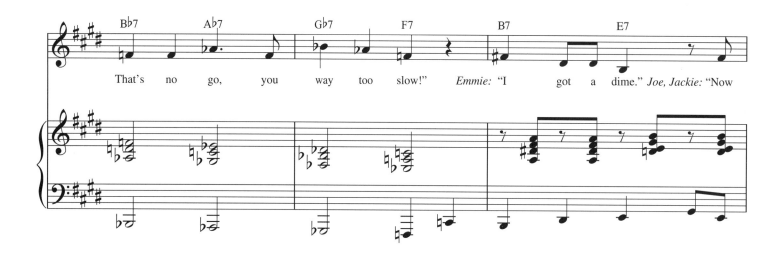

That's no go, you way too slow!" Emmie: "I got a dime." Joe, Jackie: "Now

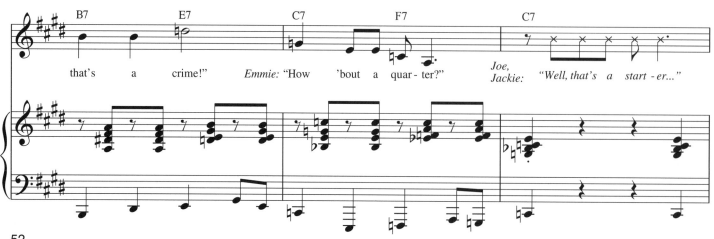

that's a crime!" Emmie: "How 'bout a quar-ter?" Joe, Jackie: "Well, that's a start-er..."

Faster (no swing)

Swing

sprout - ed wings, __ and he flew up to Heav - en and Heav - en look __ like the

Sev - en E - lev - en! Joe: And all the stars of Heav - en, they was pen - nies and dimes. __

No swing

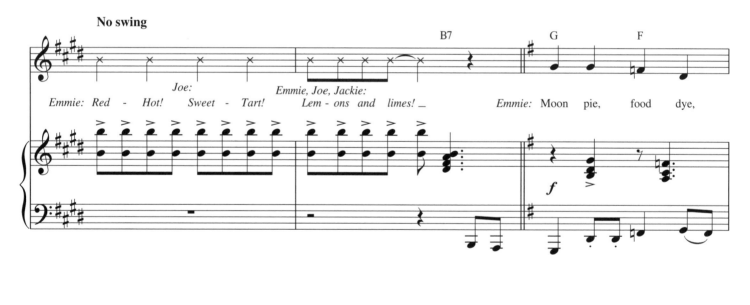

Emmie: Red - Hot! Sweet - Tart! Joe: Lem - ons and limes! __ Emmie: Moon pie, food dye,

Joe, Emmie, Joe, Jackie:

Toot - sie Pop! __ Joe, Jackie: Pop gun, squirt gun, stick - y bun, __

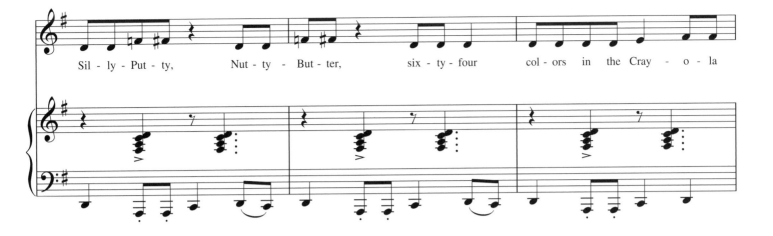

Sil - ly - Put - ty,   Nut - ty - But - ter,   six - ty - four   col - ors   in the Cray - o - la

Jackie:
pack   pack   pack!   *Emmie:* Bird   call,   slap   pad - dle,   Tin - ky - winks, __

skip   rope,   lic - o - rice,   pick - up   sticks! __   *Joe, Jackie:* Mag - ic   tricks,   Leg - o

bricks,   pi - rate   hooks   and   com - ic   books!

Noah, Joe, Jackie:
Com - ic books!
Joe: Su - per - man, Jackie: Bat - man,

Jackie: Joe, Jackie:
Joe: A - qua - man and I - ron - man, Spi - der - man, X - men, Dare - dev - il, Doc - tor Strange. And Emmie:

Noah, Emmie, Joe, Jackie:
Won - der Wom - an! Di - an - a! Prin - cess of the

Am - a - zons! Emmie: Mag - i - cal lar - i - at, gold - en ti - ar - a,

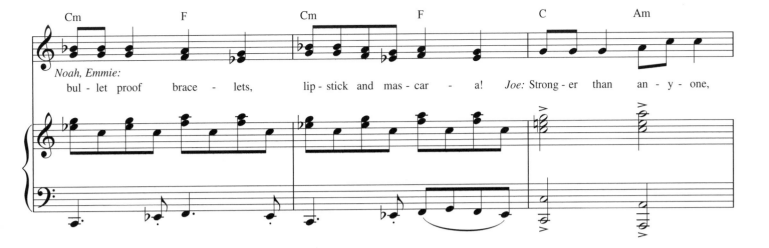

Noah, Emmie:
bul - let proof brace - lets, lip - stick and mas - car - a! Joe: Strong - er than an - y - one,

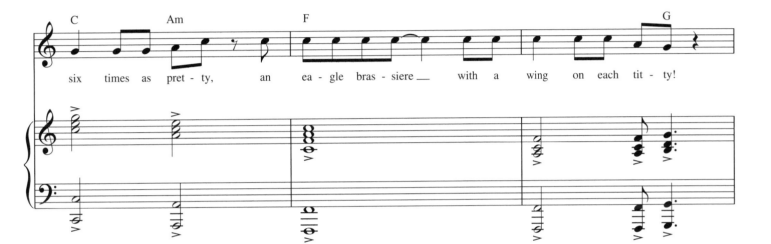

six times as pret - ty, an ea - gle bras - siere __ with a wing on each tit - ty!

Noah, Emmie, Joe, Jackie:
Wing on each tit - ty! Wing on each tit - ty! Tit - ty, tit - ty, tit - ty, tit - ty,

Freely

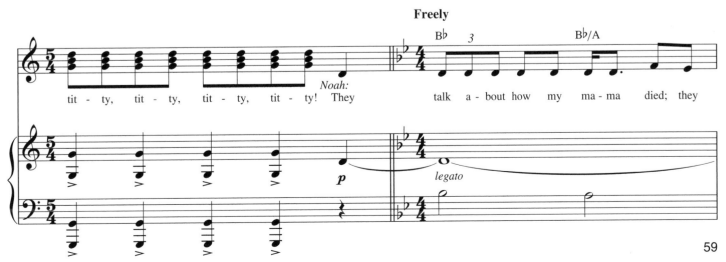

tit - ty, tit - ty, tit - ty, tit - ty! They

Noah:
talk a - bout how my ma - ma died; they

59

talk a-bout __ my trag-e-dy. __ They wish that they could take me in and

I could live with *Car-o-line __ and Em-mie, Jack-ie, Lar-ry, Joe, Em-mie, Jack-ie, Lar-ry, Joe. Each

*Pronouned *Carolyn*

eve-ning I could up and go home to be a Thi-bo-deaux. __ Em-mie, Jack-ie, Lar-ry, Joe, and

Tempo I

Tacet

No-ah, No-ah Thi-bo-deaux. ___

poco rall.

Noah, Emmie, Joe, Jackie:
Oh, __ she

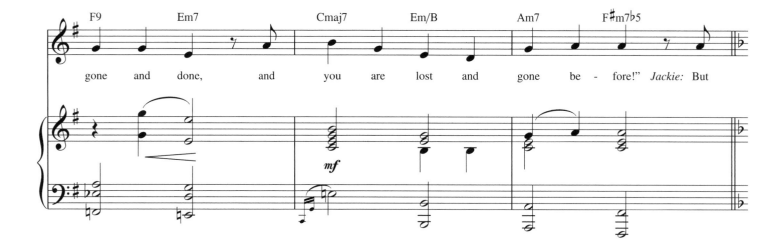

gone and done, and you are lost and gone be - fore!" *Jackie:* But

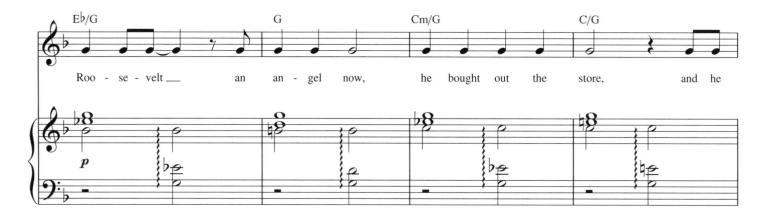

Roo - se - velt ___ an an - gel now, he bought out the store, and he

still got nick - els and dimes ga - lore! ___ His ma - ma cry, "He's gone too soon!" But

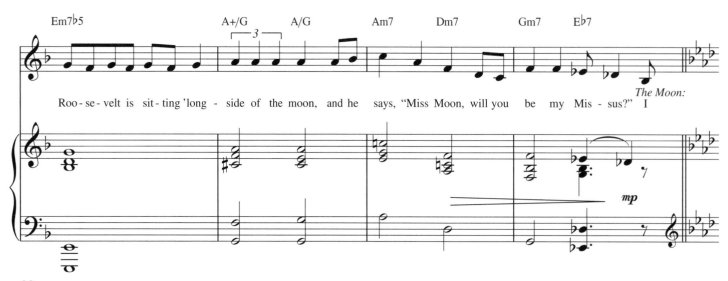

Roo - se - velt is sit - ting 'long - side of the moon, and he says, "Miss Moon, will you be my Mis - sus?" I

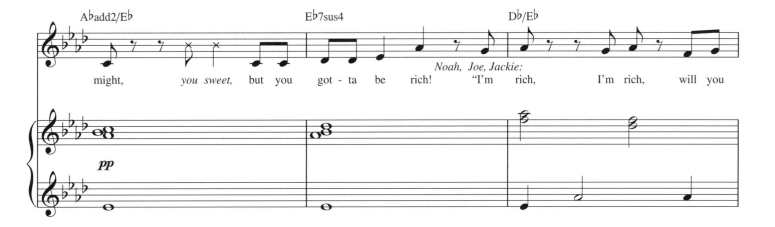

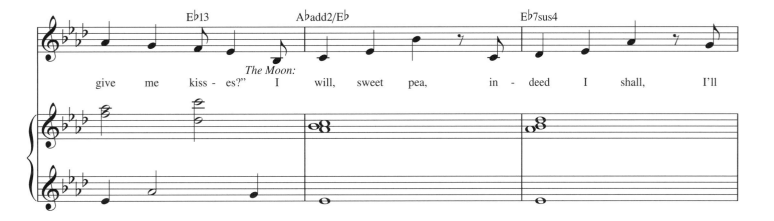

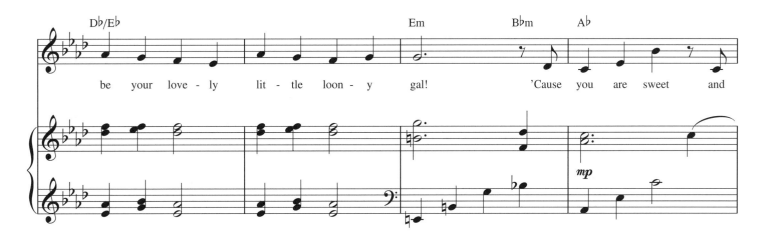

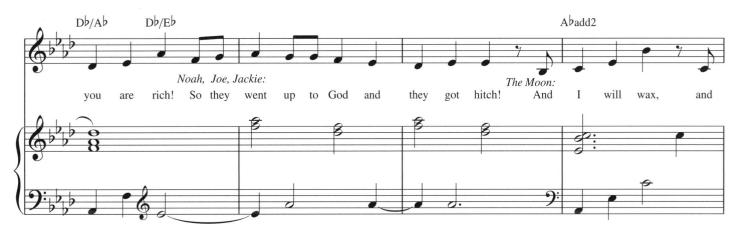

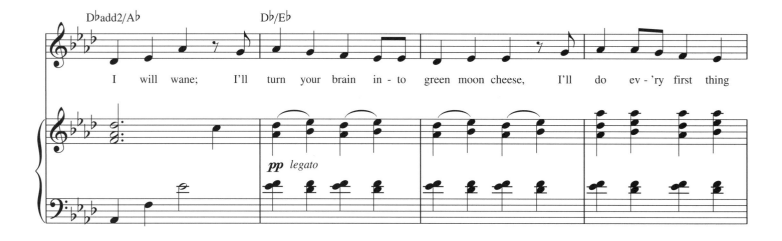

I will wane; I'll turn your brain in-to green moon cheese, I'll do ev-'ry first thing

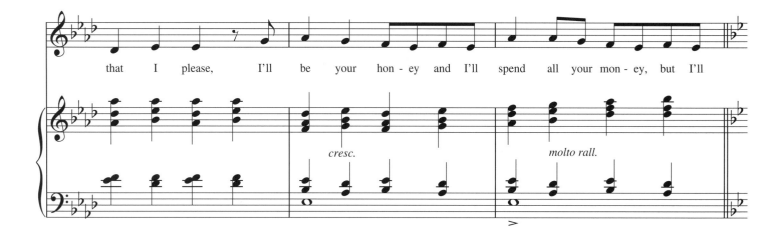

that I please, I'll be your hon-ey and I'll spend all your mon-ey, but I'll

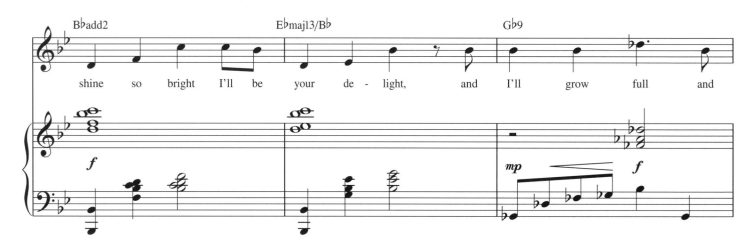

shine so bright I'll be your de - light, and I'll grow full and

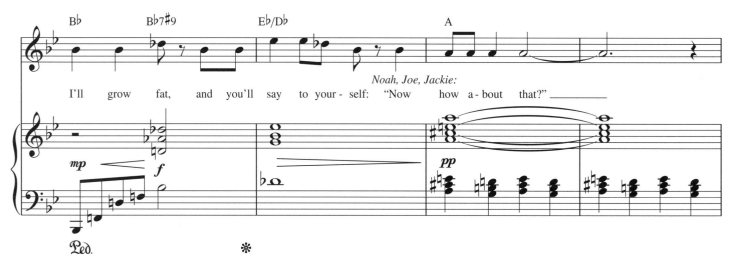

Noah, Joe, Jackie:

I'll grow fat, and you'll say to your - self: "Now how a - bout that?" _____

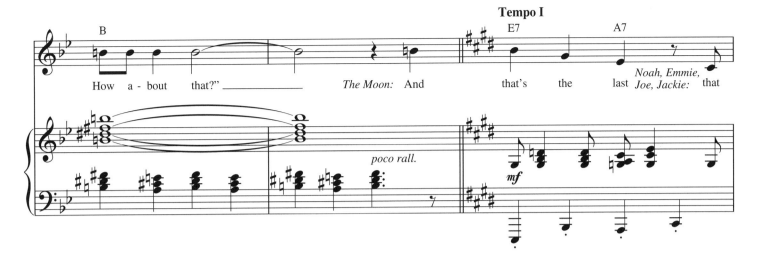

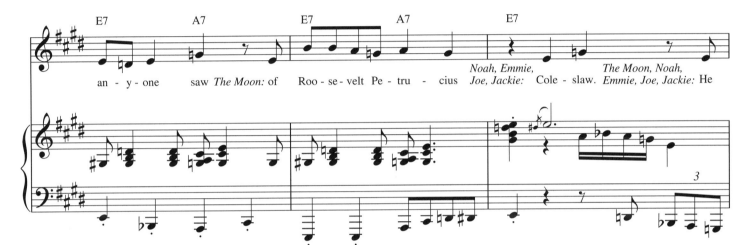

ver - y day, __ count - ing all the stars in the Milk - y Way. He

counts so high he's a mil - lion - aire __ and __ he does - n't

The Moon, Noah, Emmie, Joe, Jackie:
have a care. Ching! Ching! Ching! Ching - a - ling - a,

Caroline: And now __ ev-'ry morn - in'

I Saw Three Ships

Words by
Tony Kushner

Music by
Jeanine Tesori

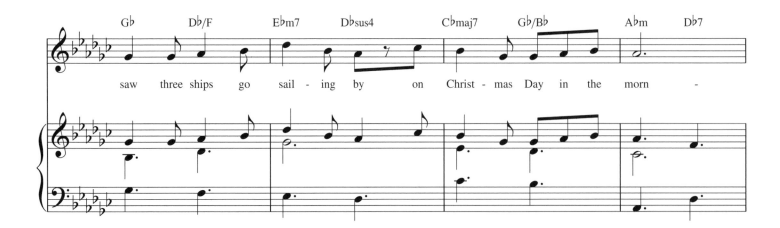

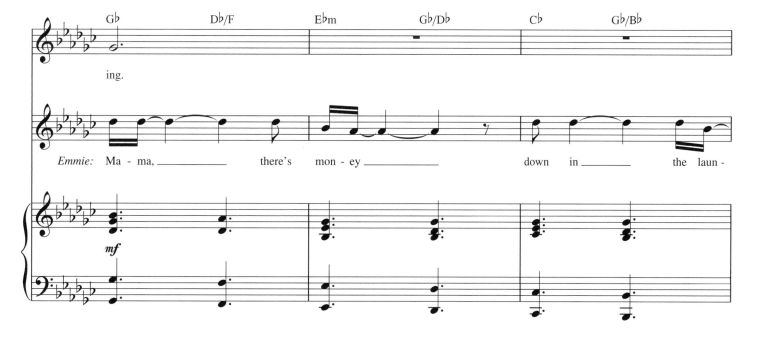

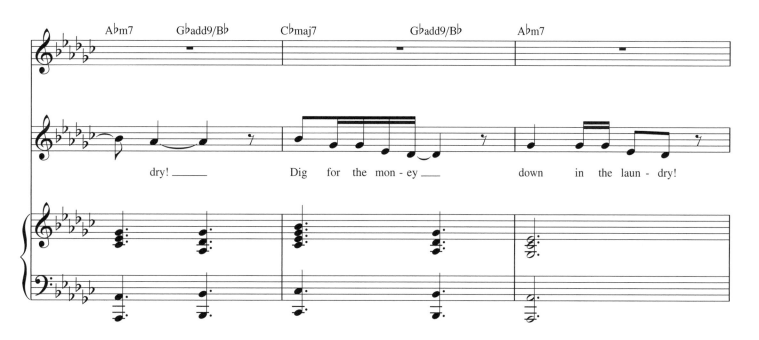

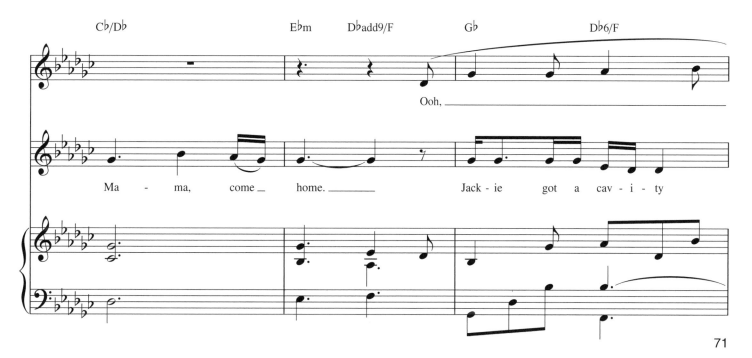

Lyrics:
eat-ing that can-dy you al-ways buy-in' now; he needs the den-tist,

and I need five dol-lars to go to Beau-mont ooh.

to see the Live Na-tiv-i-ty, and Christ-mas is com-in' and

I Hate the Bus

Words by
Tony Kushner

Music by
Jeanine Tesori

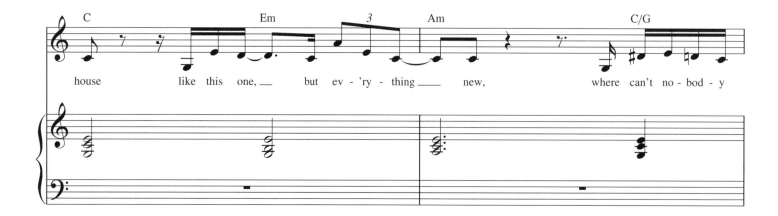

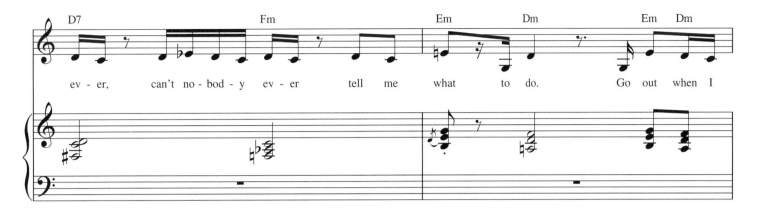

ev - er, can't no - bod - y ev - er tell me what to do. Go out when I

want to; _____ when I don't, then I stay. Got mag - i - cal

Rose: Stu - art.

Go see is No - ah al - right.

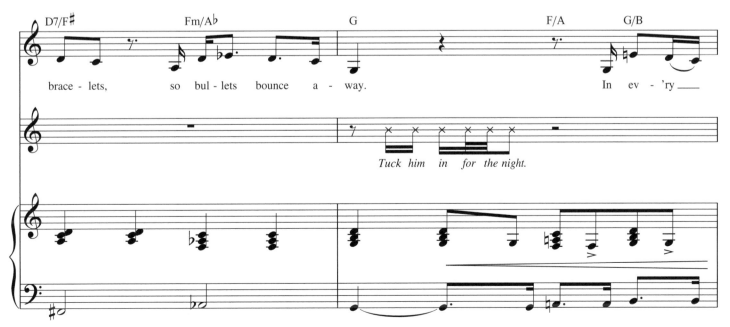

brace - lets, so bul - lets bounce a - way. In ev - 'ry _____

Tuck him in for the night.

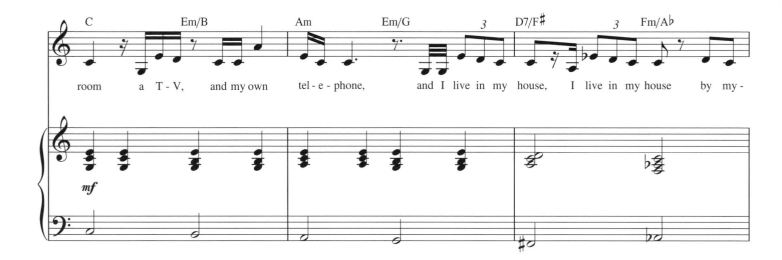

room a T - V, and my own tel-e-phone, and I live in my house, I live in my house by my-

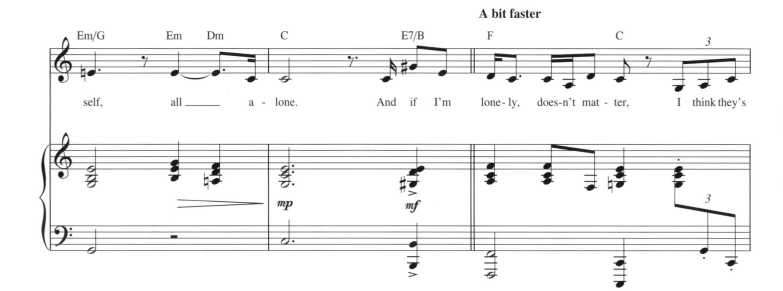

A bit faster

self, all _____ a - lone. And if I'm lone-ly, does-n't mat-ter, I think they's

worse than be-in' lone-ly. They's peo-ple who freeze ___ while they wait ___ on their knees ___ and they don't ___

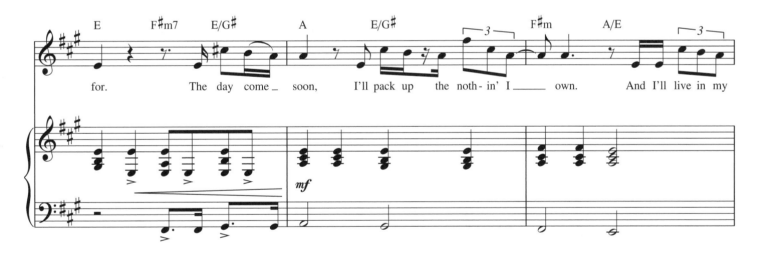

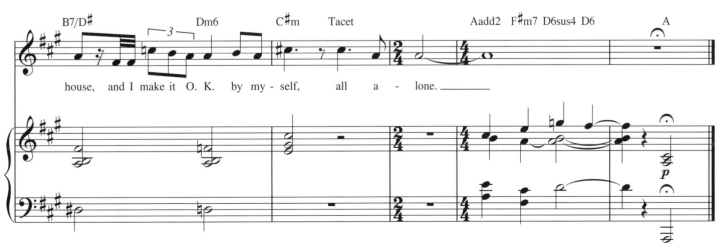

Lot's Wife

Words by
Tony Kushner

Music by
Jeanine Tesori

Slowly (in time)

Mm, _____ mm. _____ Hop-in' wa-ter turn to wine,_ hope's

fine, hope's fine, hope's fine, till it turn_ to mud._ And

some folks goes to school at nights, _ some folks march for civ-il rights._ I don't.

I ain't got _ the heart. I can't hard - ly read. _

Some folks do all kinds of things __ and black folk some day live like kings ____ and __

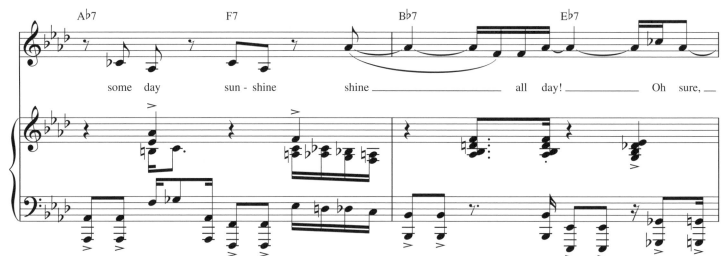

some day sun - shine shine _____ all day! _____ Oh sure, __

____ it true, __ it be _____ that way. __ But

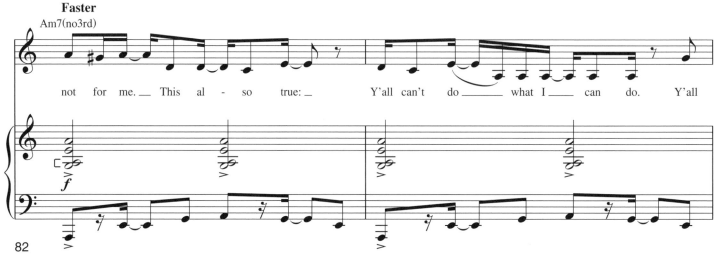

Faster

Am7(no3rd)

not for me. __ This al - so true: __ Y'all can't do _____ what I __ can do. Y'all

strong, but you ain't strong _ like me. _____ I'm gon - na

slam that i - ron down on my heart. Gon - na slam that i - ron down on my throat. Gon - na

Faster ($\flat\flat$ = $\flat$ $\flat$)

slam that i - ron down on my sex. Gon - na slam it, slam it, slam it down _

_ till I drown _ the fire _ out, till there ain't no air left an - y - where. _

What else, what else, what else, what else God,_____ what else

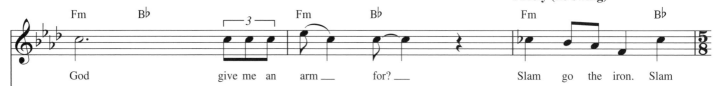

Freely (no swing)

God give me an arm___ for?___ Slam go the iron. Slam

colla voce

go the i - ron. Flat! Flat! Flat! Flat!_____

Tacet

Moderately, funky

Now how a - bout that,___

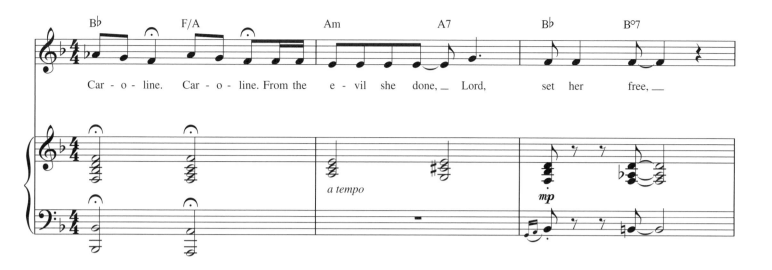

Car - o - line. Car - o - line. From the e - vil she done, ___ Lord, set her free, ___

Freely

set her free, ___ set ___ me free. ___ Don't let my sor - row make e - vil of

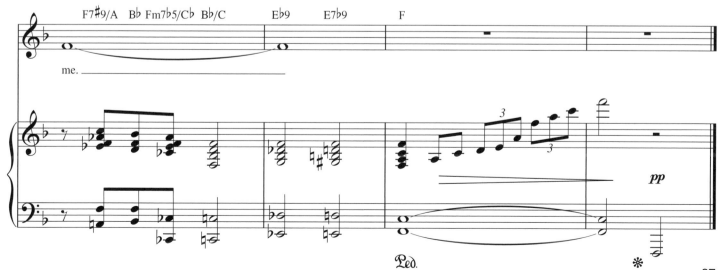

me. ___

Salty Teardrops

Words by
Tony Kushner

Music by
Jeanine Tesori

Oh, oh, oh, oh, oh. _____ Salt - y _____

Oh, oh, oh, oh, oh. _____ Salt - y _____

o - cean. _____ Oh, oh, oh, oh, oh. Salt - y, _____ salt - y tear-

tear - drops, _____ cry - in' tear - drops.

tear - drops, _____ cry - in' tear - drops.

drops; _____ I been cry - in' salt - y tear - drops un - der-

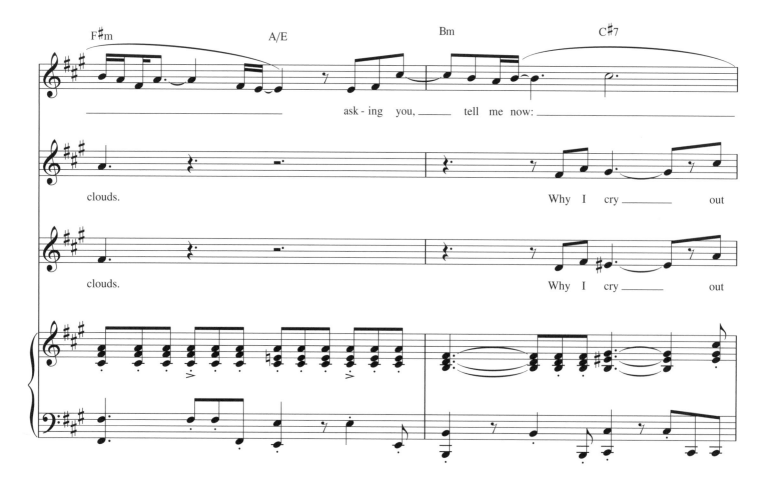

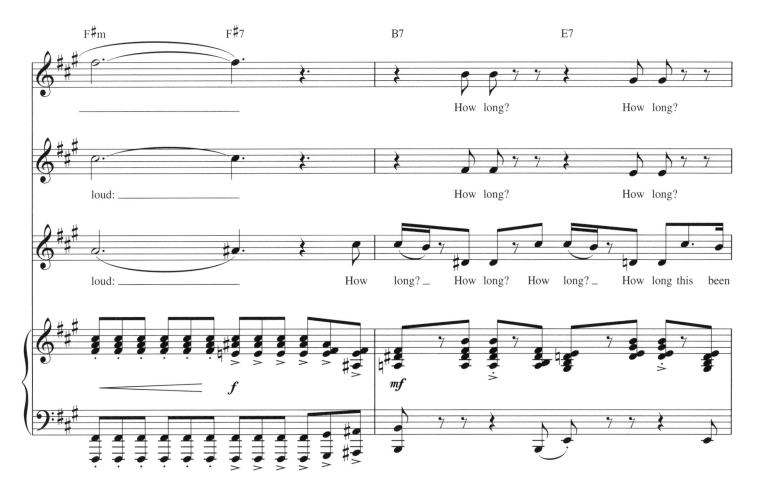

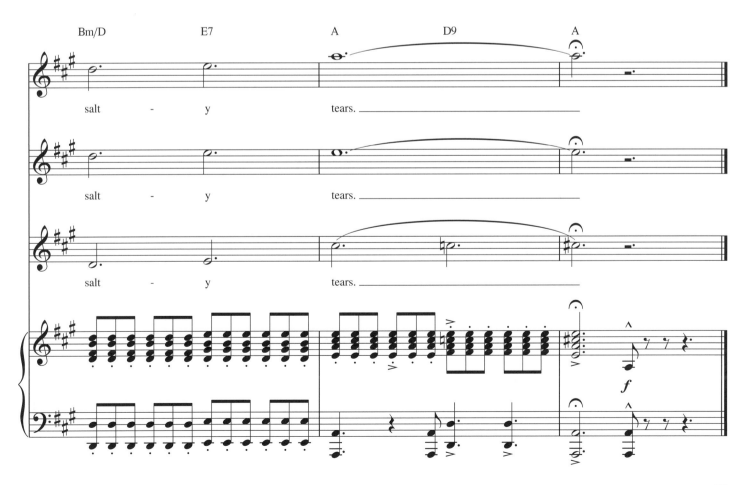

Epilogue

Words by
Tony Kushner

Music by
Jeanine Tesori

Freely (no swing)

time is past; now on your __ way. Get gone and nev – er come a – gain! For

change come fast and change come slow, __ but ev – 'ry – thing chang – es! And you got to

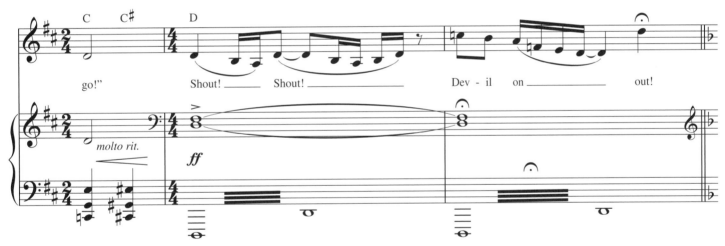

go!" Shout! __ Shout! __ Dev – il on __ out!

Slowly

Emmie: I'm the

Jackie, Joe: Ma – ma sleep – in', she work all day. __ Don't wake Ma – ma; let her sleep, __

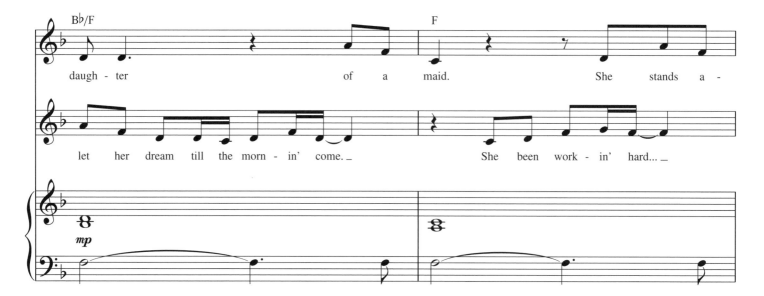

daugh - ter of a maid. She stands a -

let her dream till the morn - in' come. _ She been work - in' hard... _

A bit faster

lone where the harsh winds blow: _____ salt - ing the earth so noth - ing

grow too close; but still her strong blood flow...

Moderately slow, in 2

Un - der - ground through hid - den veins, _ down from storm clouds when it rains,

100

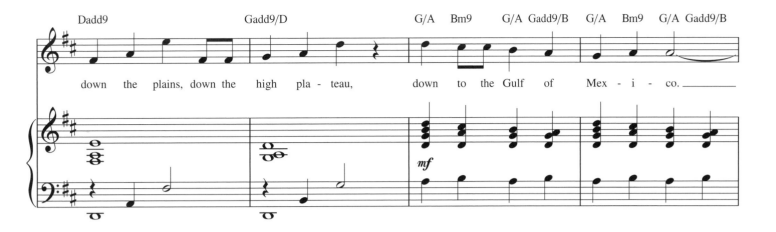

down the plains, down the high pla - teau, down to the Gulf of Mex - i - co. _____

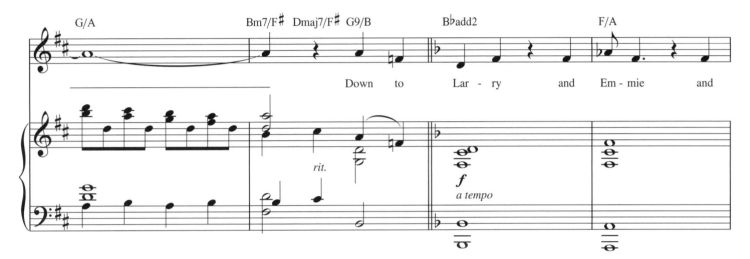

_____ Down to Lar - ry and Em - mie and

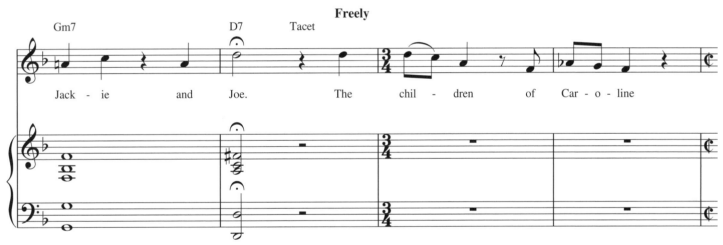

Freely

Jack - ie and Joe. The chil - dren of Car - o - line

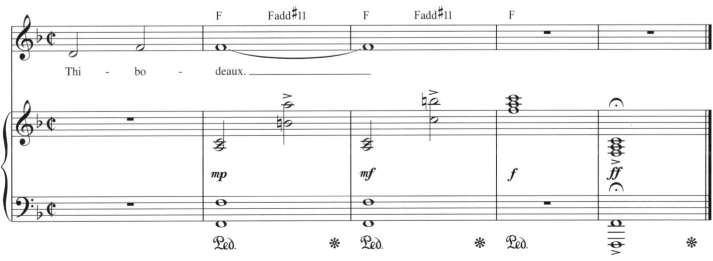

Thi - bo - deaux. _____

great songs series

This legendary series has delighted players and performers for generations.

Great Songs of Folk Music

Nearly 50 of the most popular folk songs of our time, including: Blowin' in the Wind • The House of the Rising Sun • Puff the Magic Dragon • This Land Is Your Land • Time in a Bottle • The Times They Are A-Changin' • The Unicorn • Where Have All the Flowers Gone? • and more.
02500997 P/V/G...$19.95

Great Songs from The Great American Songbook

52 American classics, including: Ain't That a Kick in the Head • As Time Goes By • Come Fly with Me • Georgia on My Mind • I Get a Kick Out of You • I've Got You Under My Skin • The Lady Is a Tramp • Love and Marriage • Mack the Knife • Misty • Over the Rainbow • People • Take the "A" Train • Thanks for the Memory • and more.
02500760 P/V/G...$16.95

Great Songs of the Movies

Nearly 60 of the best songs popularized in the movies, including: Accidentally in Love • Alfie • Almost Paradise • The Rainbow Connection • Somewhere in My Memory • Take My Breath Away (Love Theme) • Three Coins in the Fountain • (I've Had) the Time of My Life • Up Where We Belong • The Way We Were • and more.
02500967 P/V/G...$19.95

Great Songs of the Pop Era

Over 50 hits from the pop era, including: Every Breath You Take • I'm Every Woman • Just the Two of Us • Leaving on a Jet Plane • My Cherie Amour • Raindrops Keep Fallin' on My Head • Time After Time • (I've Had) the Time of My Life • What a Wonderful World • and more.
02500043 Easy Piano..$16.95

Great Songs for Weddings

A beautiful collection of 59 pop standards perfect for wedding ceremonies and receptions, including: Always and Forever • Amazed • Beautiful in My Eyes • Can You Feel the Love Tonight • Endless Love • Love of a Lifetime • Open Arms • Unforgettable • When I Fall in Love • The Wind Beneath My Wings • and more.
02501006 P/V/G...$19.95

Great Songs of the Fifties

Features rock, pop, country, Broadway and movie tunes, including: All Shook Up • At the Hop • Blue Suede Shoes • Dream Lover • Fly Me to the Moon • Kansas City • Love Me Tender • Misty • Peggy Sue • Rock Around the Clock • Sea of Love • Sixteen Tons • Take the "A" Train • Wonderful! Wonderful! • and more. Includes an introduction by award-winning journalist Bruce Pollock.
02500323 P/V/G...$16.95

Great Songs of the Sixties, Vol. 1 – Revised

The updated version of this classic book includes 80 faves from the 1960s: Angel of the Morning • Bridge over Troubled Water • Cabaret • Different Drum • Do You Believe in Magic • Eve of Destruction • Monday, Monday • Spinning Wheel • Walk on By • and more.
02509902 P/V/G...$19.95

Great Songs of the Sixties, Vol. 2 – Revised

61 more '60s hits: California Dreamin' • Crying • For Once in My Life • Honey • Little Green Apples • MacArthur Park • Me and Bobby McGee • Nowhere Man • Piece of My Heart • Sugar, Sugar • You Made Me So Very Happy • and more.
02509904 P/V/G...$19.95

Great Songs of the Seventies, Vol. 1 – Revised

This super collection of 70 big hits from the '70s includes: After the Love Has Gone • Afternoon Delight • Annie's Song • Band on the Run • Cold as Ice • FM • Imagine • It's Too Late • Layla • Let It Be • Maggie May • Piano Man • Shelter from the Storm • Superstar • Sweet Baby James • Time in a Bottle • The Way We Were • and more.
02509917 P/V/G...$19.95

Great Songs of 2000-2009

Over 50 of the decade's biggest hits, including: Accidentally in Love • Breathe (2 AM) • Daughters • Hanging by a Moment • The Middle • The Remedy (I Won't Worry) • Smooth • A Thousand Miles • and more.
02500922 P/V/G...$24.99

Great Songs of Broadway – Revised Edition

This updated edition is loaded with 54 hits: And All That Jazz • Be Italian • Comedy Tonight • Consider Yourself • Dulcinea • Edelweiss • Friendship • Getting to Know You • Hopelessly Devoted to You • If I Loved You • The Impossible Dream • Mame • On My Own • On the Street Where You Live • People • Try to Remember • Unusual Way • When You're Good to Mama • Where Is Love? • and more.
02501545 P/V/G...$19.99

Great Songs for Children

90 wonderful, singable favorites kids love: Baa Baa Black Sheep • Bingo • The Candy Man • Do-Re-Mi • Eensy Weensy Spider • The Hokey Pokey • Linus and Lucy • Sing • This Old Man • Yellow Submarine • and more, with a touching foreword by Grammy-winning singer/songwriter Tom Chapin.
02501348 P/V/G...$19.99

Great Songs of Christmas

59 yuletide favorites in piano/vocal/guitar format, including: Breath of Heaven (Mary's Song) • Christmas Time Is Here • Frosty the Snow Man • I'll Be Home for Christmas • Jingle-Bell Rock • Nuttin' for Christmas • O Little Town of Bethlehem • Silver Bells • The Twelve Days of Christmas • What Child Is This? • and many more.
02501543 P/V/G...$17.99

Great Songs of Country Music

This volume features 58 country gems, including: Abilene • Afternoon Delight • Amazed • Annie's Song • Blue • Crazy • Elvira • Fly Away • For the Good Times • Friends in Low Places • The Gambler • Hey, Good Lookin' • I Hope You Dance • Thank God I'm a Country Boy • This Kiss • Your Cheatin' Heart • and more.
02500503 P/V/G...$19.95

cherry lane
music company
www.cherrylane.com

Prices, contents, and availability subject to change without notice.

0812